Sports Illustrated Kids: Legend

LEBRON JAMES

VS.

MICHAEL JORDAN

BASKETBALL LEGENDS FACE OFF

by Dionna L. Mann

CAPSTONE PRESS
a capstone imprint

Published by Capstone Press, an imprint of Capstone
1710 Roe Crest Drive, North Mankato, Minnesota 56003
capstonepub.com

SPORTS ILLUSTRATED KIDS is a trademark of ABG-SI LLC. Used with permission.

Library of Congress Cataloging-in-Publication Data is available on the Library of Congress website.

ISBN: 9781669079705 (hardcover)
ISBN: 9781669079651 (paperback)
ISBN: 9781669079668 (ebook PDF)

Summary: LeBron James and Michael Jordan are basketball superstars! Between the two, James has more playoff appearances, but Jordan leads in NBA championships. So which one is the all-time best? Young readers can decide for themselves by comparing the fantastic feats and stunning stats of two legendary pro basketball players.

Editorial Credits
Editor: Christopher Harbo; Designer: Sarah Bennett; Media Researcher: Svetlana Zhurkin; Production Specialist: Katy LaVigne

Image Credits
Associated Press: Kirthmon Dozier, 10, Susan Ragan, 13, Tom DiPace, cover (right); Getty Images: Allsport/Jonathan Daniel, 5, 15, 16, 18, Brian Bahr, 9, Christian Petersen, 14, Harry How, 19, Jason Miller, 6, Jonathan Daniel, 23, Kirk Irwin, 17, Los Angeles Times/Wally Skalij, 12, Matthew Stockman, 7, Mike Ehrmann, 22, 26, NBAE/Nathaniel S. Butler, 29, Ronald Cortes, 8, Ronald Martinez, 4, Steph Chambers, 11, Thearon W. Henderson, 28, Tim Nwachukwu, 25; Newscom: ZUMA Press/The Palm Beach Post/Allen Eyestone, 21; Shutterstock: saicle (background), cover and throughout; Sports Illustrated: John W. McDonough, cover (left), Manny Millan, 20, 24, 27

Printed and bound in the USA. 5853

CONTENTS

* * * *All stats are current through the 2022–2023 NBA season.* * * *
Words in **bold** appear in the glossary.

Basketball Legends Face Off!

Michael Jordan and LeBron James are NBA superstars. Jordan played 15 seasons before **retiring** in 2003. James has played 20 seasons and counting. Both have been called the greatest of the game. But who is the best? You decide!

LeBron James

Michael Jordan

THE MATCHUP	Born	State
Jordan	1963	New York
James	1984	Ohio

Nothing But Net

Great players like James and Jordan always score lots of points. To date, James has an **average** of 27.2 points per game during his **career**. But Jordan inches him out. He averaged 30.1 points per game.

James shoots for the Los Angeles Lakers.

Jordan takes a jump shot for the Chicago Bulls.

THE MATCHUP	Average Points Per Regular Season Game
James	27.2
Jordan	30.1

Two-Pointers

Basketball is a game of twos. Every **layup**, jump shot, or slam dunk adds two points to the scoreboard. So far, James has landed 11,891 regular season two-pointers. Jordan made 11,611 during his career.

James scores against the San Antonio Spurs.

Jordan makes a layup in a game against the Detroit Pistons.

THE MATCHUP	Regular Season Two-Point Field Goals
James	11,891
Jordan	11,611

Slam Dunk Contests

Basketball gets really exciting when players slam dunk. "Air" Jordan seemed to fly while dunking. During his career, he took part in three NBA Slam Dunk Contests. He won two. "King James" has slam dunk power too. But he has yet to take part in an NBA Slam Dunk Contest.

Jordan dunking during an NBA Slam Dunk Contest

James throwing down a powerful dunk during a game

THE MATCHUP	Slam Dunk Contest Wins
Jordan	2
James	0

Steals

A well-timed steal can turn the tide of a game. Both James and Jordan have had the moves to strip the ball away. James has 2,186 regular season steals. But Jordan has him beat. He had a whopping 2,514 steals!

James steals a pass in a game against the Denver Nuggets.

Jordan steals the ball in a game against Angola during the 1992 Olympics.

THE MATCHUP	Regular Season Steals
James	2,186
Jordan	2,514

Blocking

Basketball isn't all about scoring points. Sometimes a **block** can be the difference in the game. So far, James has averaged 53.65 blocks per season. Jordan's average was higher. He had 59.53 per season. That's a lot of blocking!

James stops a shot by the San Antonio Spurs.

Jordan jumps to block a shot by the New York Knicks.

THE MATCHUP	Average Blocks Per Regular Season
James	53.65
Jordan	59.53

Rebounds

In any given NBA game, less than half the shots swoosh through the net. That's why great ballers are always ready to **rebound**. Both Jordan and James have been rebound pros. Jordan snagged 6,672 rebounds during his career. So far, James has grabbed 10,667.

Jordan grabs the rebound in a game against the Utah Jazz.

James snags a rebound in a game against the Oklahoma City Thunder.

THE MATCHUP	Regular Season Rebounds
Jordan	6,672
James	10,667

Playoff Games

Only the best teams make the **playoffs**. Both James and Jordan have been on their fair share of winning teams. Jordan played in 179 playoff games with one team. James has played in 282 playoff games with three teams.

Jordan in action during a playoff game against the Atlanta Hawks

James taking a jump shot in a playoff game against the Golden State Warriors

THE MATCHUP	Playoff Games Played	Teams
Jordan	179	Chicago Bulls
James	282	Miami Heat, Cleveland Cavaliers, Los Angeles Lakers

Playoff Assists

NBA superstars own the spotlight during the playoffs. But Jordan and James's playoff **assists** prove they are team players. Jordan made 1,022 assists during the playoffs. But James is in the lead with 2,023 assists so far!

Jordan passes during a playoff game against the New York Knicks.

James attempts to pass to his teammate during a playoff game against the Philadelphia 76ers.

THE MATCHUP	Total Playoff Assists
Jordan	1,022
James	2,023

NBA Championships

Every year, two teams battle their way to the NBA Finals. But only one can be crowned a **champion**. So far, James and his teams have played in 10 NBA Finals and won four! Jordan's team played in six and won every time!

James dunks during the 2020 NBA Finals against the Miami Heat.

Jordan protects the ball during the 1997 NBA Finals.

THE MATCHUP	NBA Finals	Wins
James	10	4
Jordan	6	6

All-Star Invitations

Each year, the best players are **invited** to play in the NBA All-Star Game. Jordan was invited to 14 All-Star Games out of 15 seasons. James has 19 All-Star Game invitations out of 20 seasons.

Jordan playing in the 1993 NBA All-Star Game

James dunking during the 2022 NBA All-Star Game

THE MATCHUP	NBA All-Star Game Invitations
Jordan	14
James	19

MVP Awards

The NBA hands out its **MVP** awards at the end of every season. To date, James has four regular season MVPs. He also has four NBA Finals MVPs. Jordan earned five regular season MVPs. He had six NBA Finals MVPs.

James holding his 2012 NBA Finals MVP trophy

Jordan receiving his 1992 NBA Finals MVP trophy

THE MATCHUP	Regular Season MVP	NBA Finals MVP
James	4	4
Jordan	5	6

Face Off Winner?

After looking at their stats, did you pick a face off winner? Was it James because he tops Jordan in two-point shots and playoff assists? Or was it Jordan because he had more steals and championships? What did you decide?

LeBron James

Michael Jordan

Glossary

assist (uh-SIST)—a pass that leads to a basket by a teammate

average (AV-uh-rij)—a number found by adding a group of figures together and then dividing the sum by the number of figures that were added

block (BLOK)—a move that stops a pass or shot

career (kuh-REER)—a person's main work over a large part of their life

champion (CHAM-pee-uhn)—the winner of a competition

invite (in-VITE)—to ask to do something or go somewhere

layup (LAY-up)—a close shot where the ball is gently played off the backboard and into the hoop

MVP (EM-VEE-PEE)—short for most valuable player

playoffs (PLAY-awfs)—a series of games played after the regular season to decide a championship

rebound (REE-bound)—to take possession of the ball after it bounces off the backboard or rim

retire (ri-TIRE)—to give up a line of work

Read More

Greenberg, Keith Elliot. *LeBron James vs. Michael Jordan: Who Would Win?* Minneapolis: Lerner Publications, 2024.

Hubbard, Crystal. *Who Is LeBron James?* New York: Penguin Workshop, 2023.

Sarantou, Katlin. *Michael Jordan.* Ann Arbor, Mich.: Cherry Lake Publishing, 2021.

Internet Sites

Jr. NBA: About the Game
jr.nba.com/category/about-the-game/basketball-basics

National Geographic Kids: Bonkers About Basketball
natgeokids.com/uk/kids-club/entertainment/general-entertainment/bonkers-about-basketball

Sports Illustrated Kids: Basketball
sikids.com/basketball

Index

About the Author

Photo by Dionna L. Mann

Dionna L. Mann is a children's book author and freelance journalist. She spent more than 25 years volunteering and working in the school system where her talented children attended. Dionna's favorite part of working with children was teaching them about writing and reading their heartfelt words. As a person of color, she enjoys learning about lesser-known people found in the records of African American history. You can find Dionna online at dionnalmann.com.